The Woman's Blueprint

Elizabeth D. Wallace

THE WOMAN'S BLUEPRINT by Elizabeth Wallace

Published by Createspace, an AMAZON company

Unless otherwise indicated, Scripture quotations are taken from the New King James Version of the Bible. Copyright © 1979, 1980, 1982 by Thomas Nelson, Inc. Used by permission. All rights reserved.

Scripture quotations marked ESV are from the Holy Bible, English Standard Version. Copyright © 2001 by Crossway Bibles, a division of Good News Publishers. Used by permission. All rights reserved.

Scripture quotations marked NIV are from the Holy Bible, New International Version. Copyright © 1973 1978 1984 International Bible Society. Used by permission. All rights reserved.

Cover Design: Janiel Jkheck
www.fiverr.com
Editor: Flora Brown
Foreward: Carmela S. Williams
Copyright © 2016 by Elizabeth D. Wallace
All rights reserved.

Library of Congress Cataloging-in-Publication Data
Wallace, Elizabeth D

The Woman's Blueprint / by Elizabeth D. Wallace
ISBN-13: 978-1537138091
ISBN-10: 153713809X

Printed in the United States of America

This book is dedicated to my family:

To my husband, Lorenzo Wallace, whose unconditional love and support inspires me to strive for greatness and comforts me when I miss the mark.

To my parents, Ladson and Louella Jackson, whose unwavering guidance and encouragement gave me the foundation to be a woman of excellence.

To my sons, Dana and Eusebio, you are the reason I do what I do. I am so honored to be your mom and love you more than words can say.

ACKNOWLEDGMENTS

To everyone that had any input into my life that lead me to write this book, I acknowledge you and hold you close. It is because of you, I am able to begin the journey of writing and use the gifts that God has bestowed upon me. I am particularly grateful for everyone that provided insight, resources and wise counsel that brought this book to completion.

Contents

Foreward

Nothing is off limits in this book. From the very beginning you will come face to face with your own self-limiting beliefs. Do you believe you are good enough? Do you believe you are beautiful? Do you believe you can grow? Do you believe in your gifts, skills and abilities? Do you feel inferior? You will quickly come face to face with the things that are robbing you of your peace, health and ultimate success. In the introduction section, Elizabeth begins to speak positive affirmations into your life. No seriously, she really speaks them and it flows like rivers of living water. After the first page, I started to squirm in my seat because I began to ask myself is this true about me. I had to slow down and reread the affirmations again so that I could digest them all. It was as if my big sister was having a conversation with me about life.

You will find that Elizabeth is speaking to you in a very straight-forward, conversational manner. Everything is discussed from finance, to limiting beliefs, to family, to diversity, to forgiveness, to playing in the dirt. You will go deep into every area that makes us unique women. As I read through each chapter, I felt like I had a tour guide through life. Imagine planning a trip to an unfamiliar place. In preparaing for the trip, you read books and watch videos to familiarize yourself with the natives and their culture. Before departure, you discover you will have a personal tour guide leading you through the unfamiliar areas of your journey; what an added sense of security. You do not have to travel alone. As women, there are places in our lives that we have compartmentalized and hung a sign that says "closed for repair." We decided that life is okay with that area closed off and any time we find ourselves in a place where someone tries to enter our closed zones, we disconnect. Elizabeth serves as a guide to reconnect those closed-off barren places. She not only tears down the "closed for repair" signs but she walks us through the remodeling phase and empowers us to declare "Open for Life." Once you go through this new journey of self discovery, healing and wholeness, you will find yourself ready to embrace new opportunities, to make new memories and serve in new capacities.

I've known Elizabeth for 18 years and I have watched her live this blueprint. I have seen her go through the self-discovery phase. I have witnessed the brokenness and the restoration. I have seen her as a caregiver to her family and as a leader within corporate America. I have seen her make the right decisions and not just the popular ones. I have experienced her wise counsel and her total surrender to God's plan for her life. The Woman's Blueprint is perfect for this season and generation. This book is essential because we are in a historical time for women. It is a time when a woman has been accepted as the Democratic nominee for President of the United States. Whether you have accomplishments of women such as Condoleezza Rice, Michelle Obama and Hilary Clinton or the uncertainty of a teenage mother or the anxiousness of a high school senior, this book is the perfect next step for you. The **only** requirement is to be ready to go to the next season in your life.

The Woman's Blueprint is a detailed outline or plan of action. Many books tell you why but Elizabeth takes it a step further by walking us through the process of "how." How do I forgive? How do I achieve a healthy balance of my physical, mental and spiritual self? How do I balance my dream and reality? The How is just as important as the Why. At the end of each chapter, you will have the opportunity to reflect and put an accountability plan in place through the Empowerment Techniques section. This was my favorite part of the book because you have a safe place to gather your thoughts and immediately apply that section to your life. It helps you discover how you will move forward. When you complete this book, you will not have Elizabeth's blueprint for being a woman but you will have developed your own customized blueprint for success. Once you look back through each chapter you will discover that you have written a step-by-step plan for your own growth. You will have discovered, rediscovered or expanded on the woman you were destined to become. You will have celebrated your possibilities and learned from your challenges as you embraced your very own Blueprint.

Carmela Williams

Pastor, Author, Singer & Certified Coach, Speaker & Leadership Trainer
Vidalia, Georgia

Introduction

This book is created FOR YOU, and at NO TIME reading this book are you allowed to think negative in ANY sort of way, nor can you let negativity into your sphere. You should go to a relaxing spot where you curl up with a good book, preferably THE WOMAN's BLUEPRINT and emerge into what it has to offer.

The purpose of this book is YOU and how to become the best version of yourself so that you can live an abundant life. You can consider me your BFF, bestie, that girlfriend you've known since grade school. The college roommate you shared all of your thoughts and dreams with and in the end became your "sister from another mother." This book is for you, so collect your favorite throw, pour a glass of your favorite wine, slip into something comfortable as we review, discuss, and evaluate The Woman's Blueprint. Now as your bestie, let me do my job and celebrate you for being the Woman you are and the Woman you will become. Here we go....

You are Beautiful. You are thoughtful. You are my best friend, and I support you. I've learned a lot from you. I've seen you grow so much. I like spending time with you. You are fun to be with. You bring out the best in me. You are a fantastic person. You are a hard worker. You are so smart. I value your insight. You have a lot to offer. I really admire your inner strength. You are (will be) an amazing mother. I don't know what I would do without you. I'm amazed at the woman you've become. You have accomplished a lot. I'm grateful that I can trust you with anything. I have total confidence in you. I respect the woman you are. My hat's off to you! You've got great ideas. I rely on your intuition. I can face anything with "My Girl" by my side. You are the best woman I know. I really appreciate your loyalty. You are a great cook. You are so creative. You are one talented woman! You never stop giving. You look fabulous in that outfit and have impeccable taste. You work hard to make things wonderful for everyone around you. You are a unique person. You are a conqueror. You got what it takes to make things happen. You impress me, you really do! You are a woman of integrity. I admire you. I'm proud of how you handle situations. You're a solid rock and I love your spine of steel. You are a considerate person. Thank you for making so many ordinary moments, extraordinary. You help me make my half-hearted attempts more whole-hearted through kindness, commitment, and teamwork. You're a keeper. I appreciate your honesty. You are a blessing. You encourage me to be someone special. Your words heal, and not wound. Your smile is contagious. You look great today. You're a smart cookie. You have impeccable manners. I like your style. You have the best laugh. I appreciate you. You are the most perfect you there is. You are enough. You are strong. Your perspective is refreshing. You are an awesome friend. You light up the room. You deserve a hug right now. You should be proud of yourself. You're more helpful than you realize. You have a great sense of humor. Your kindness is a balm to all who encounter it. You are all that and a super-size bag of chips. On a scale from 1 to 10, you're an 11. You are brave. You are even more beautiful on the inside than you are on the outside. You have the courage of your convictions. You are making a difference. You're like sunshine on a rainy day. You bring out the best in people. Your ability to recall random facts at just the right time is impressive. You are a great listener. You always look great, even in sweatpants. Everything would be better if more people were like you! You are cooler than a fan. That color is perfect on you. Hanging out with you is always a blast. You always know -- and say -- exactly what I need to hear when I need to hear it. You smell really good. You are an amazing dancer! Being around you makes everything better! I believe in you. You are not afraid to be yourself and you are incredible. Colors seem brighter when you're around. You are so interesting. You are wonderful. You tell funny jokes. Your hair looks stunning. You have the perfect set of eyes. You are one of a kind! You are inspiring. You should be thanked more often. So thank you! You build people up, when life knocks them down. You have the best ideas. You always know how to find that silver lining. You never quit. You always get back up and keep going. You are a candle in the darkness. You are an example to others. You are a wise woman. I trust you. You always know just what to say. You're always learning new things and trying to better yourself. You are more fun than bubble wrap. When you make a mistake, you fix it. You're a genius at figuring stuff out. Your voice is magnificent. The people you love are lucky to have you in their lives. You're like a breath of fresh air. You're gorgeous. Your creative potential seems limitless. You are a force. You are intelligent. You are a heart-centered woman. You are a Fashionista. You are a

Woman of Zion. You are a merchant ship. You are a Teacher. You are a life-saver. You have a beautiful voice. You are an achiever. You have a loving spirit. You are worth it. You are graceful. You are magnificent. You are a great Wife. You are an asset to any occupation. You bring a lot to the table. You can start any business you desire to have, and you will be successful. Actions speak louder than words, and yours tell an incredible story. When you make up your mind about something, nothing stands in your way. You seem to really know who you are. Any team would be lucky to have you on it. There's ordinary, and then there's you. You're someone's reason to smile. You're even better than a unicorn because you're real. You have a good head on your shoulders. Has anyone ever told you that you have great posture? The way you treasure your loved ones is incredible. You're really something special. You're a gift to those around you.

Chapter 1

SELF

Most works of literature are written to build up to the plot of the story or conclusion which signifies the point the author is trying to convey. You generally have to read well into the 4th Chapter to find out the "secret." Fortunately, I am not good at

> **SELF** - *a person's essential being that distinguishes them from others, especially considered as the object of introspection or reflexive action: (google.com)*

keeping secrets, so I am going to share the purpose of this book up front.

It is how the things you deal with in your everyday life impacts you and how you can leverage it to work in your favor. In discussing YOU, we will talk about you in great detail. So let's start off with SELF... yes, your SELF, my SELF, our SELVES, **SELF**. Dictionary.com defines self as a person's usual or typical bodily make-up or personal characteristics; the distinct individuality or identity of a person or thing. My definition of self, is an internal designation comprised of traits, thoughts, and personalities that are derived from characteristics, innate and learned behaviors, and experiences.

Growing up, I can recall my mother saying, "Behave your SELF, look at your SELF," and my favorite, "think for your SELF." Although my mother meant well, none of these comments provided a good reflection of my "SELF." In today's world, we are taught to Self-reflect, visualize a positive Self-Image, and be your Authentic Self. I agree with all of it, but the question is how? How do I change my negative past and create a renewed Image of myself? How do I escape the controversy or conversation of yesterday by changing how I see my SELF in the mirror? In this book, we are going to explore techniques together to help us do just that! Change how we see our SELF.

As a young girl growing up in South Georgia, I struggled to fit in. Although I was considered "smart," I camouflaged my insecurities by an overcompensating amount of arrogance. I was often criticized for thinking that I was better than everyone else when actually I felt everyone was better than me. I had secrets, doubts, fears, and no one to confide in or share them with. I was the only girl in my family and eldest of my cousins... so I had to be a role model, even if it was a façade. As a result, I unknowingly developed a distorted view of how I saw myself, which followed me into my late 30's. It influenced my perception, relationships, education, career choices, and how I mothered my children.

You see, the perception of my SELF was wrong and disingenuous. It prohibited me from being a true friend and a committed partner. My Self Image was so skewed that I was in denial about my own physical appearance and how others perceived me, even down to my family. I thought they saw me as a strong independent woman, but after many heartfelt and hurtful conversations, they revealed the witch that I had become. I was sharp, rude, insensitive, and sometimes inappropriate in how I spoke to and treated them, but if you had asked me, I would have described myself as direct, truthful, and no-nonsense. Do you see how a misguided self-image affects you and everyone around you?

Although this is just one of many examples I experienced on my road to redemption and/or authenticity, it is not unlike your story. You may not have had the same experiences, but you too have built up walls of untruths that have painted an inaccurate picture of who you really are and how it's impacting every valuable relationship, and decision in your life. Together, we will learn how to tear down those walls, determine if walls are needed and rebuild them with doors and windows, so that you can let the individuals that are worthy enter into your circle.

Walls

Did you know that walls are a direct result of your past experiences? Maybe you were neglected, experienced parental alienation, compared to others, suffered as a victim of a violent crime, experienced or watch someone be domestic and/or sexually abused, misused, or abandoned. There are so many negative experiences that created the walls that you wear as a trophy and display to the world. Until recently, I thought that everything bad that happened in my life, on some level, was my fault and that I had done something wrong, and as a result, I was being punished.

As an adult, our childhood beliefs follow us and dictate our actions, which can serve us well when we are 8, 9, even 12, but as we age, our belief system can cause much of the pain and suffering we experience on a daily basis. The author of Renovate, shares that we respond to life with bad behaviors because they are based on False Beliefs. The author also recommends that we discard those false beliefs and replace them with positive ones. As our mind conjures up thoughts, we have the opportunity to either believe the thought or disregard it as a false idea. Disregarding negative thoughts not only increases awareness but generates empowerment.

You may have heard the battle begins and ends in the mind. Since many of us haven't realize that every thought that comes into our mind isn't true and haven't learned how to discern our true voice, we are crippled from deciphering genuine beliefs from false ones. For example, as a child, we are taught that if we received good grades in school, our parents would be proud of us. As we continually operate under that conceptual framework, we develop the belief that we require approval from others. This belief can become debilitating because without approval, we would be unable to accomplish tasks or complete assignments. It also hinders us from becoming an independent individual.

"Hi, my name is Maggie, and I have a Self-Image problem." Having a self-image issue is similar to an addict; whether it is alcohol, drugs, or any other activity that alters the mind. It impacts how you think or perceive yourself. If your self-image is negative, it compounds the impact and causes damage to you and others around you. An alcoholic can go to AA meetings for assistance, but where do individuals like you and me go for wise counsel or help. Most of us learn to cope or internalize our self-issues. In doing so we become stagnate, withdrawn, and oblivious to how life really should be for us. That's why it is so important for the transformation to begin internally and in the mind as it will eradicate all effects of a negative self-image.

Empowerment Technique

In an effort to distinguish false beliefs, you must first identify when and how your mind tells you an untruth (a lie). Take an objective look at your inner thoughts. Journal the thoughts or conversations you have internally with yourself. ~~Cross out the negative thoughts~~ to destroy their energy and power over you and highlight the positive thoughts for agreement.

Example: I received an invite to a friend's restaurant opening 2 months ago. A month prior, I purchased a really cute dress for the event. Since that time, I experienced some dietary setbacks and gained more than a few pounds. The day before the event, my mind began to do a number on me, impacting my behavior and ultimately my family.

<u>False Belief (FB) vs. Empowering Belief (EB).</u>

> *FB – You know you are NOT going to be able to wear that dress you bought. Even if you can get in it, it's not going to be flattering on you. You've gained too much weight. EB – It will be fine, just try the dress on. If it is snug, you're a seamstress and can alter the dress.*

> *FB – Why wear a dress you have to alter? Plus, you don't have the time for that... not only do you have to prepare your clothes, but the family EXPECTS you to make their clothes as well.*

> *EB - You got this! Hubby can wear a black suit; the boys can wear a shirt and slacks... no worries.*

Now you give it a try and write your belief conversation below, remembering to ~~cross out the FBs~~ and highlight the EBs.

_____

_____

_____

_____

The importance of the above exercise is to strategize internally on defeating the inner culprit that tries to boggle, confuse, and hinder your growth. Fortunately, we are going to discuss many options to thwart this damaging mindset. To sum it up, identifying the FBs from the EBs is vital to your future.

Chapter 2

Forgiveness

When I look at you, I see a Woman of strength, truth, honor and beauty. You are the embodiment of integrity, who anyone and everyone can trust in. You are a woman of wisdom and stature, who has favor with God and man. There isn't anything you can't do... except FORGIVE.

Wow! what an exception to an outstanding pedigree! Have you ever heard, "Hell hath no Fury like a Woman Scorned"? This reference still holds true today, but it is not a good thing. You can become a woman scorned if you have been hurt by a jilted lover, a neglectful parent, or a betraying friend. Whatever the situation is or was; instead of forgiving the offender, the Scorned Woman chooses to bask every day in corrosive anger and revolving resentment. Instead of making a decision to free herself and live in peace that surpasses all understanding, she prefers to rot in deliberate anguish and personal defeat. Do you know anyone like this? Are you that woman?

The nature of forgiveness is being able to have compassion for those who have wronged you opposed to harboring ill emotions, such as anger, resentment, vengeance or spite against them.

Not too long ago, this woman was me. I was invited to a friend's house along with 8 other women. We ate dinner, played games and talked about mutual interest. Throughout the night I noticed the host taking pictures of her guests. In one instance, she asked me to lean away while she took a photo of the woman sitting next to me. As the night went on, she never asked me to pose for a picture and at the end of the night I felt excluded. On my way home, I wondered why she did not include me in the picture. I even thought, she could have taken the picture and deleted it once I left, if she really didn't want to commemorate my attendance at her home.

Several more thoughts frolicked through my mind on my journey home but by the time I went to bed, I had chosen to forget about it. Then the next day came and I was awakened by a call. When I saw her name on the caller ID, all of the emotions from the night before resurfaced, but this time with some additional feelings. Immediately, I thought to myself; what does she want? Why didn't she call one of the women she took pictures of last night? So reluctantly, I answered the phone and pretended to be asleep. She apologized for waking me and asked if I was available today for a quick outing. I replied that I was not and would have to catch her next time. At first, I thought I would "get over" my feelings but instead they began to consume my thoughts whenever she was around or her name was mentioned. I began to dodge her phone calls and avoid running into her in common circles. I started to have internal conversations on how to address this with her. I even tried to role play the exchange with my husband. At first I thought I wanted to just talk it out with her because she may not have realized how she made me feel until I saw her Facebook page and there they were; all of the pictures she had taken without ME! The emotions were back with a vengeance. How could something so trivial impact me to this degree and why had it invaded my peace to this magnitude. I soon decided that I preferred peace over strife. Not only did I forgive the act and the actor but I forgave myself for playing co-star.

After going through the experience I realize the agony I put myself through wasn't worth it. The experience did not put me in a situation that I couldn't recover from. In fact, no one has that power over me; unless I give it to them.

You may question that I don't understand what has been done to you or that your situation was irreversible. The ability to grant forgiveness is beyond your capabilities because the offender caused hurt and harm. You are right. I don't know your struggle, but in my experience, I have come to realize it is best to forgive.

Forgiving someone does not mean you forget the offense that occurred or excuse it. The very act of forgiving is more for you and your own personal growth. You substitute your negative thoughts with positive feelings, thoughts, and behavior and make the choice to show them generosity, compassion, and kindness. What you receive in return is Freedom. Freedom, from the awkwardness, from the pain, from the fear, even freedom from the experience.

Empowerment Technique

Take a moment and write down situations or events that are still incarcerated in your heart with revenge or resentment. Then write a statement to those events that will result in growth opportunities for you. Similar to the first exercise, ~~cross out~~ the incarcerated situations of resentment or revenge to destroy their energy and power over you and highlight the positive thoughts of forgiveness and freedom for confirmed empowerment.

Example: I shared a private experience with a longtime friend. This experience left me feeling insecure and unsure of myself. I hadn't had the nerve to share this with anyone else for fear of judgement and ridicule; but my friend was very supportive and encouraging. She even shared an embarrassing experience that impacted her life. After speaking with my friend I felt relieved that I had found a confidant. Two months later, I was out to lunch with a mutual friend who shared that she was sorry to hear about my past experience and if I ever needed to talk she was always available. I immediately asked for clarification as to what she was referencing and ~~she recanted what I shared with my friend~~.

Incarcerated with Revenge/Resentment (IR) vs Forgiveness and Freedom (FF).

IR - I felt betrayed by my friend and started down the cycle of anger and revenge.

IR - I could have exposed my friends secret or slander her for violating trust and being a gossipier.

FF – Deciding not to provide energy to the situation.

FF – Deciding to forgive in spite of the betrayal but learned the level of trust I had with my friend.

_____

_____

_____

_____

Chapter 3

Equipped for the journey

"Health is the state of complete physical, mental, and spiritual well-being."

With all of the news highlights, exercise videos and cooking shows, the secret is out that wellness is much more than physical health, exercise and/or nutrition. It is a complete combination of physical, mental, and spiritual well-being. Since there are many books on physical wellness, we will not cover it here. We will however, discuss techniques for mental, social, emotional, and spiritual wellness; each of these components infused together contributes to our personal quality of life. **Now before I can share my thoughts and experiences with you, I must share that all content found in this book was created for informational purposes only. The content is not**

intended to be a substitute for professional medical advice, diagnosis, or treatment. Always seek the advice of your physician or other qualified health provider with any questions you may have regarding a medical condition. Never disregard professional medical advice or delay in seeking it because of something you have read in this book.

Below is a brief definition of each property of wellness.

- *Mental Wellness is a state of well-being in which the individual realizes his or her own abilities, and can cope effectively with the normal stresses of life.*
- *Social Wellness is the ability to establish and maintain positive relationships through relating and interacting with people.*
- *Emotional Wellness is the ability to acknowledge and share positive and negative feelings in a productive manner.*
- *Spiritual Wellness is the ability to establish harmony between our values, beliefs, and actions that equate to our life purpose.*

Pack Your Suitcase

It is easy to advise you on how to pack and what to wear on a trip to the Bahamas, the Alps or Paris, but complete wellness is an individual prescription, and one size does not fit all. Most people will advise you to start with the physical, but your physical is an outer reflection of what's going on internally. For you to begin to understand the nature of your health, you would need to recognize and identify your own personal needs. The next few paragraphs will provide you with the least invasive but highly effective techniques of the Wellness properties.

Mental Wellness

We all have unique needs, and it's important to identify your needs. My friend Lois shared with me, as a young girl in grade school, she was considered "smart" and excelled without trying. She managed to graduate from high school and college with little effort. She even went on to work for the federal government. As she grew older, it became difficult for her to retain information and she struggle with simple reasoning. She often experienced severe brain fog and was unable to focus on any one task for a long period of time. She was challenged with simple life stresses and dwelled on small, insignificant things. At one point, she started to have negative centered thoughts and calamity based dreams; so she went in to get professional help. She was diagnosed with ADD (Attention Deficit Disorder), and this started her journey of understanding her abilities and how to positively deal with life issues; good and bad. Lois's experience is unique to her, but it's not unusual. Mental Health and wellness is important at every stage of life, from childhood to adolescence to adulthood. It also helps us to determine how we handle stress, relate to others, and make choices. Over the course of your life, you may experience mental health concerns, which could affect every aspect of your life. Mental health issues are common and with the **proper** care you can get better, if not recover completely.

Empowerment Technique

I empower you to implement gradual changes by taking small steps. Many mental health problems begin when physical stress or emotional stress triggers chemical changes in your brain. The objective is to reduce stress and restore normal chemical processes in your brain. Managing your mental health helps you to deal with stressful situations effectively. In other words, you'll be in a position to live a happier, healthier life in a way that is malleable, enjoyable, and free of judgment or discipline. Learning and maintaining good coping skills will take practice but will become easier over time.

Here are a few techniques that can assist with maintaining Good Mental Health.

- *Meditation and Relaxation: Deep breathing techniques or progressive muscle relaxation can help to reduce stress and induce relaxation.*
- *Physical Activity: 20-30 minutes of exercising for at least 4 days is a method of stress relief.*
- *Humor: Laughter is food for the soul and is unquestionably an effective technique for stressful situations.*
- *Pets: Taking care of a pet helps to distract the mind from stressful thoughts.*
- *Sleep: The human body requires rest to repair itself after a stressful day.*

Take a moment and write down your coping skills on how you deal with stress. As a reminder, good coping skills help to establish good mental health wellness.

_____

_____

_____

_____

Social Wellness

Social health is the positive interaction with others that impacts your mental and physical health. When you are socially healthy, you have the skills to socialize, be confident and function in all situations while building relationships with other people. If you lack social wellness, you tend to lack the ability to adjust to social situations.

An old friend of mine, Darlene, recently shared that she felt uncomfortable around people, even people she had known for years. When she found herself alone in close quarters with other folks, she struggled to find something to talk about, in most cases, she let the awkward silence fill the space. As a result, the situation never allowed her to get to know others or for them to get to know her. Ultimately, people would shy away from her because she was perceived as a recluse. Interestingly, Darlene is not alone, many women shy away from a crowd or defer to the next person instead of leading the conversation. One of the greatest things that you can do for yourself and others is to become a contributing member in conversations and in your community. The more you motivate yourself to get out and join many different activities, the more you contribute to your social health. Volunteer work is a good place to start. You can find these types of activities through your church, by asking friends, reading your local newspaper, and searching the internet. Going through the day having positive interactions with other people will provide you with a great deal of social wellness. So go out into your community and make a difference! I must pause here to share that social wellness is not the same as being "on social media," while you maybe "friending" people, you are not creating intimate relationships that require personal contact and spending time with close friends.

To sum it up, social wellness is the positive effect friends have on your mental and physical health. It is a measure of your health based on the number of close, personal friends you have, how often you spend time with them in person, and how often you make new, lasting friendships. One rule to remember, you get out what you put in. So give yourself to others and reap short and long term rewards.

Empowerment Technique

I empower you to close down the computer or app to your social media sites. Reach out to a friend that has been longing to spend time with you or review the events/activities going on around town and plan to attend. Use this opportunity to practice your social skills by observing and befriending one person from each event.

Here are some steps that can help you to create social wellness:

- *Give of yourself – take the initiative to offer friendship to others. Join clubs, associations, and groups that share the same interest.*
- *Choose your friends wisely - Get to know people to decide if they are "worthy" to be your friend; this will ensure that the friendship is positive for both parties.*
- *Learn to build and stay in healthy relationships - these relationships involve people you care about*

and who care about you and your well-being. *Generally, these are people whom you feel can nurture and support your needs and whose needs you yourself can offer support to. By establishing trust and compassion, you will feel safe and satisfied; two vital ingredients for social wellness.*

- *Have confidence in your uniqueness - Realize that your friends do not have to be like you, although you may have things in common. Everybody's different and true friends not only accept it, but they also celebrate it.*
- *Foster effective communication - it is important that your friendships have open 2way communication. For all parties to grow, you must be able to provide insight, guidance, and support through the good and bad times... truthfully; once this is established, you will have a healthy and mature friendship.*

Take a moment and write down your coping skills on how you interact socially. You can use the above social cues to create a strong foundation for social wellness.

_____

_____

_____

_____

Emotional Wellness

Emotional wellness enables you to maintain fulfilling relationships, deal with conflict, and remain grounded during demanding times. This wellness property is one of the hardest to bring in alignment and to maintain. It can cause just as much; if not more havoc in your life than physical wellness. Most of us have experienced daggers to our self-esteem, rejection, failure, and loss of a loved one or pet companion. Experiencing anyone of these situations can send you on a downward spiral to doom and gloom and sometimes it takes years before you recover or gain a sense of normality (feeling like your old self).

Recently, my family went through a traumatic experience that changed our lives forever. My eldest son took a friend to meet someone. Shortly after their arrival, 2 young men got into an altercation and as a result, my son (while standing by his car) was shot 4 times. When I learned of the situation, my heart fail to the floor. By the time, I got to the hospital, they had taken him back for immediate surgery because his injuries were life threatening. Prayerfully my son survived, but the events sent me on an emotional roller coaster. I experienced all the stages of grief. I couldn't sleep. I couldn't eat. I lost weight. I became paranoid; I didn't want the boys out of my site. I couldn't focus enough to cook, clean or work.

Yes, we were blessed that our son survived, but the incident left me afraid and angry. Not necessarily at him; but at myself, because I didn't teach him the ability to discern friend from foe, and how to be aware of your surroundings and detect trouble. My emotional health was a train wreck, and because I hadn't slept, I wasn't sure if I was coming or going. When I was alone, I would have a crying outburst. Whenever I tried to work, I would stare at the computer. Since my son almost lost his life, I was annoyed by the smallest complaints of insignificance and didn't want to be around people. When I did go to my personal spaces or engage in things that I like doing, like rubbing my dog, writing, or even praying, I struggled to focus. As the weeks went by, I finally realized that my emotional state needed professional help. Help, to make it through the day. Help to go to sleep at night. Help to cook for my family. Help to move past the tears. So I did; I got help.

Your traumatic experience may not be as bad as mine or it may be worst; the truth is, trauma and/or loss is a natural part of life, and none of us can avoid it. Regardless of how painful or traumatic the experience, what is important for emotional recovery and overall wellness is to find a reason for the incident or a lesson learned. When we can define the good from the experience, the healing process begins. It can also serve as a greater appreciation for family and friends. A mindset change or a shift may occur in your values and morals, or it can sharpen your survival instincts and create preparedness for future events. For me, our situation set off emotional triggers to let me know that my emotional well-being was in jeopardy.

Although, in the initial stage of my experience, I felt helpless and lost the motivation to do everyday tasks. So to regain my emotional composure, I made a list of all of my blessings and the things that were under my control. I praised myself for being a supportive mother to my sons. I thanked God for enabling me to hug my son and receive a hug back. I constantly spoke affirmations to myself and aloud. I focused on praying and helping others so that my mind was not constantly thinking about my own situation.

Empowerment Technique

I empower you to distract yourself from gloomy thoughts, as soon as the thought begins, arrest it and engage it in a task that requires concentration. Surround yourself with a positive support group. Having friends who are willing to listen and support you through this season of your life is paramount and can be the saving grace of how you grow through the experience.

Here are some extra things that can help to you sustain and maintain emotional wellness:

- *Stay positive – it is important to focus on the positive. Healing powers are in positive thoughts.*
- *Eating healthy – Eat the things that will fortify your body and provide proper nutrients for strength and nourishment.*
- *Rest – Sleep is when the body heals itself, so get plenty of rest.*
- *Physical Activity – concentrating on your physique will provide a break from the emotional stress you are undergoing.*
- *Spirituality – get in tune with divine powers. Allow yourself to bask in his fullness for true restoration.*
- *Connect and help others – the best feeling is when you help others. This will allow your mind to rest from your current situation and focus on helping someone else.*
- *Take time for yourself – most important prescription is to spend time with you for focus and clarity.*

Take a moment and write down your coping skills on how you maintain a strong foundation for emotional wellness.

_____

_____

_____

_____

Spiritual Wellness

This property is by far one of the most important properties that influence every aspect of your life as well as the people around you. Some of us would say that they do not believe in God or the spirit realm, but the moment you ask, "why am I here?" "What am I meant to be?" "What is my purpose;" you have become aware of your spirituality.

Your spiritual wellness plays a great importance to your overall health than you may believe. It is the method that ignites you to seek and receive answers to the things that spike your curiosity as it relates to spiritual matters. Understanding **YOUR** spirituality will motivate you to achieve unimaginable things whereas; spiritual atrophy can motivate you to do unspeakable things.

To be clear, when we are talking about spirituality, we are talking about the core essence of you, the inner workings of you, the entity that defines you, dictates where you come from, your destiny, and the path that will help you reach your goals.

When we start the journey of Spiritual Awareness, we become Seekers. A seeker begins by asking themselves spiritual base questions. Sometimes the awareness is brought on by an experience; generally traumatic and life changing. It kindles the desire to interact with others or engage in different experiences to satisfy the curiosity of "what is my role in life, what was I meant to do." In the pursuit for answers, some of us look for spiritual guidance in places of worship, from pastors, ministers, and other members of their faith. If the individual is considered credible, you will often settle for the small portions of wisdom and knowledge they share with you. If you remain a seeker, you will feel the need to have others define your level of spirituality. For example, all of us know someone that are aware of their spirituality. However, when it comes to making a decision, they are stuck unless outside guidance is received.

About 14 years ago, my friend Niecy, was presented with three different opportunities. In the first opportunity, Niecy was asked to speak at a local YMCA to a group of young entrepreneurs. The second opportunity was to write an article regarding Women in Business and the third opportunity, was an invitation to the local radio station to promote her business. At first, Niecy was excited about the opportunities and how they were coming so fast. After a moment of surrealism, she said, "I don't think I can do any of these, I am not sure I have what it takes. I should call my mentor to help me decide which one is right for me." For Niecy, this was a high pressured situation but what could her mentor say to her, that she didn't already know or wasn't already doing? Please do not misunderstand; reaching out to your mentor is a good idea, but NOT to make a decision for you. The issue I found with Niecy's statement (and I told her) was that she doubted her ability to make a decision on her own.

Niecy was stuck in the beginning phase of seeking her spirituality. At that time, she struggled with the entity that defined her and described why she exist. Although we all start at the beginning in seeking the answers to our spirituality; to escape the need for outside endorsement, we must continue to further our pursuit of the meaning of life. Our quest will eventually reveal that we do not need to rely on others' interpretation to understand the source of our motivation, decisions or purpose. What do I mean? First, we all start out as Seekers, and the goal is to surpass the awareness of spiritual health to an awakening of Spiritual Wellness. This metamorphosis occurs when you realize that you can be the conduit for change in your life. In that AHA moment, you release all fear, limitations, doubt, and judgment out of your consciousness, and you become a Creator.

As a creator, you do not require outside intervention in governing yourself, your family or your life situations. The ultimate satisfaction or the ability to live an abundant life comes when we stop seeking external corroboration and learn to look internally for our answers. 2Peter 1:3 ESV shares that His divine power has granted to us all things that pertain to life and godliness, through the knowledge of him who called us to his own glory and excellence.

The ability to move from Seeker to Creator is in your approach. Seekers approach life from the outside in, while

Creators approach life from the inside out. Therefore, in your spiritual wellness journey, it is important to address your mindset. Whether or not you believe in "*As a Man Thinketh*" "*You reap what you sow,*" "*Universal Law,*" or "*Change your Brain, Change your Life,*" they are true. As Creators, we understand that we must guard our minds and our mouths; if you think bad things, you will be bad, if you sow bad thoughts, you will reap bad actions, the Universe will send you what you put out. If you change the way you think, you will change your life... period!

When life issues present themselves, we need to look internally first and then if necessary, seek wise counsel. The counsel is just that, it is an example that we listen to, apply what is applicable, and discard what we do not need. Being a creator affords us the opportunity to manage our emotions, discipline our thoughts and words, and call to surface characteristics, as we need them. In a nutshell, we have everything we need internally to live an abundant life.

We just have to conceive it, believe it, and achieve it.

Empowerment Technique

I empower you to realize that all you need to succeed in life is already inside of you. You have the confidence, talent, knowledge, and time to accomplish whatever you desire. Your spiritual awareness has freed you to be YOU, the most important person you will ever need to know.

Take a moment and notate the age-old questions, who am I, what am I meant to be, and what is my purpose? Then take a moment; think deep and answer those questions.

_____

_____

_____

_____

Chapter 4

Buried Treasure

Skills, abilities, talents, gifts are all words we use to describe things we do well. According to the dictionary, a talent is a natural ability of a person. My definition – a talent is a natural born skillset that is mastered to create an extraordinary outcome; it can be due to passion, knowledge, repetition or experience. It can manifest in creativity, athletic abilities, speaking, relationship building, and influencing others to name a few. These innate abilities are part of who we are and separate us from others. Have you ever seen or heard someone speak and their voice sounded so calming and commanding at the same time? You left feeling empowered, challenged, and motivated to complete their call to action. Later on, you find out that the individual only rehearsed the speech once or not at all.

They were anointed or blessed with the talent to speak, and since they operated in their gift, it resonated with you and left a positive impact. That is exactly what operating in your gift looks and feels like. The great news is, we all have talents, and some of our talents are easily recognized while the rest of us have to search to find out what our special abilities are; in other words, discover our buried treasure.

"There's nothing in the world like buried treasure and people hungry and obsessed enough to risk their lives for it."
Brad Meltzer

I started writing poetry when I was 13 years old. It was a way to express my frustration, confusion, pain, and joy. I wrote late at night under the covers by the light from the hallway. I wrote at school, church, in the car; wherever there was a pen and a piece of paper, I would write. It was not until college that I was asked to write for other people. I wrote resumes, CVs, essays, term papers, church programs, and poems for special life moments and each time, I was reminded that I should have been a writer. Some background... it is important to share that I had a way with words, but I was not an English scholar, nor did I know the style of my writing. I knew how to put words together on a page to create an emotion, provide a visual or share an experience, which enabled the reader to see the event or relate to the situation. That was my talent and as life continued, I received more opportunities to share my gift of words. So I began to compile my thoughts and years later, 3 books of poetry were born.

Buried Treasure

As women, we are dynamic beings, so realizing our talents may be a challenge, especially for those of us that have more than one talent. Just like buried treasure, talents are often buried beneath habits, the needs of others, jobs, and internal challenges. In order to seek out your talent, it must become a committed quest. One that requires you not only to look inward, but also listen to what other people are sharing with you. This is one of the few times when confirmation about what you should be doing comes from external sources. Your talent would be the activity; which people claim you do well. It's an accolade that follows you, regardless of the audience. It generally doesn't require a huge amount of effort from you, AND you like doing it. Your talent is different from a learned behavior. You can take your talent and learn how to master it, but it may take years to master a learned behavior. We have all heard the saying, "you can be anything you want to be if you try hard enough" and if you believe that American myth, you may be able to live a modest life. Don't get me wrong, you must work to achieve an abundant way of living, but when you are operating in your talent, work doesn't seem like work at all. Most of us have not discovered our talent or we discount it. In order to live the abundant life, we were created to live, introspecting is necessary. For example, when Misty Copeland began dancing at a young age, she excelled within a short period and began performing professionally in just over a year: a feat unheard of for any classical dancer. Misty was anointed, blessed, born to dance ballet, and because she knew it, the universe opened up for her. My point is, when your talent manifest and you operate in it, you set the stage to achieve goals like none other. Your life plan becomes in alignment, and you set the stage to live life abundantly.

Discovering your talent

Society's propaganda and marketing has hoodwinked us from birth. Parents are focused on teaching ABC's instead of finding out what we are naturally drawn to. They sign us up for sports, gymnastics, ballet, and choir, not knowing if we have rhythm or if we can even sing. They believe the rhetoric about going to school, conform to the "norm"; getting good grades so that you can go to college. Upon graduation, interview to get a good job. Again, the individual is lost in the quest to assimilate into the American Dream. It's no wonder we are unaware of our talents and gifts. I believe that children should be exposed to as many things available and out of that exposure, talents may be revealed. In an interview, around 14 years of age, Serena Williams displayed her confidence for the game of tennis; she shared that she was going to beat her opponent. At 14, Serena knew that she was operating in her talent and understood what that power meant to and for her. Even now as a young woman, she operates in that same mindset... and you can see the results.

So how do you break from the "matrix", so that you can realize and operate in your GOD giving talent? If I asked you to share the things you do well naturally, how will you respond? Most of us struggle to answer this question. Remember when I shared that we were dynamic? Our talents play a role in that attribute. In order to break free, we must become introspective; to be specific, we need to operate from the inside out. We must defer all rationale to our inner voice, our internal space, or (my reference) our spirit woman. In the confinements of our mind, the spirit woman will speak to us about our authenticity through thoughts and feelings. It demands that we release earthly limitations and self-defeating habits and/or comparison traps in order to embrace a purpose driven life. In this heart filled conversation, we are urged to move from a place of egocentric, lack, and a society driven justification to an understanding of our core abilities and talents. For example, our spirit woman will say, "when we are singing, this is who we truly are and when we perform, we are at our best." This alignment with spirit also aligns you with Source energy and being. The universe will show up with her brother the Law of Attraction to bring to you all things deserving, thus releasing you from the matrix. Now all you have to do is continue to operate in your talent, without hesitation or procrastination, and your life will change for the better.

Empowerment Technique

I empower you to have an intimate conversation with your Spirit Woman, so that you can realize and operate in your talent. I assure you, her desire for you is to feel a sense of peace and belonging, when doing what you're supposed to do. The key to living life abundantly is operating within your talents, skills, and abilities, but also doing it for yourself and on your terms.

Take a moment and write down the talents derived from

the life changing conversation. Now in order of priority,

label the talents that can be put into action quickly. This

will signify to the universe that you are ready to operate

from a place of personal power and alignment.

_____

_____

_____

_____

Chapter 5

Permission

Last week I was waiting for my youngest son to come out of the grocery store, when a little girl, about 8 years old approached me with a box of girl scout cookies. "Ma'am, would you like to buy some girl scout cookies?" Before I could respond, she rattled off the different assortments available. "I would, but I don't have any cash," I replied. "Ok," was her response as she ran to ask a lady going into the store. I watched her ask customers coming and going for the next 10 minutes. A few no's and a couple of yeses, the little girl continued on. As my son was returning to the car, I heard "thank you so much." I looked over, and a gentleman was buying a box full of girl scout cookies. Good for her, I thought, all her hard work has paid off.

During the drive home, I thought about the little girl's persistence and determination to get the job done as well as her gratitude for the people that contributed to her goal. As little girls, we wore persistence and determination like a badge of honor. Whatever we set our sights on, we asked for it. If the first answer was no, we would try again; even if it meant changing our MO or parent to get the item we wanted. As Women, we have shied away from asking for what we want, even to the point of having anxiety or just afraid to ask. Somewhere along the way we became closed mouth, tightlipped and just a downright cowardice.

Work Environment

We are hesitant to speak up and out, even if our comments could save the company money. Even though we deserve it, we are afraid to ask for a raise or promotion because of budget concerns. In our own businesses, we do not charge appropriately for quality work, and won't hesitate to provide a discount for those seeking a deal.

The real problem is not that you are afraid to speak up for yourself? It is that you don't value yourself enough to believe that you deserve what you are asking for or if you are worthy of the price. Every time you discount your services or fail to speak up, you are allowing your customers, co-workers and managers to devalue you. Does that make sense? Sort of? Let me put it another way. All of the unpaid time and uncollected monies you are giving away to your job and/or clients is being taken from your family. **HOW COULD YOU LET THAT HAPPEN?** They deserve better than the tired, bitter, unappreciated woman they currently receive day after day and night after night. To add insult to injury, you are sick of being overworked, bitter from undercharging, and you feel unappreciated from being underpaid. *You* deserve better.

You deserve to be valued, appreciated, and compensated appropriately. James 4:2 (NIV)... shares you have not because you ask not; Matthew 7:7 (KJV) shares, ask, and it shall be given unto you. If you require external confirmation, the above two verses along give you the authority to pursue top dollar for your time and expertise. You do not need to feel guilt, anxiety or frustration about respecting yourself and requiring everyone else to do the same. In fact, it would be a grave disservice to them for you NOT to, but in case you need it, here is your permission to be valued.

Home

We continue to give, provide, comfort, and cater to our family and friends even though we feel unappreciated, taken for granted or worse; making us sick. I understand that we do things for our family and friends in the name of Love... but to truly display REAL love, you must Love yourself first. You disagree? Well look at it this way, how can you teach your family self-respect, respect, honor, confidence, boundaries, and love without showing them through demonstration. Setting the example begins at home and most of the time, it starts with YOU. Let me be clear, I am not talking about the kind of love that resembles selfishness, but the kind that imitates responsibility. The responsibility to instill in everyone that you impact that because you love yourself, you can love them. Once these characteristics are learned, it applies to all areas of your lives and all your experiences.

Empowerment Technique

I empower you to realize that all you need to succeed in life, is already inside of you. You have the confidence, talent, knowledge, and opportunity to accomplish whatever your desire. Your spiritual awareness has freed you to be YOU, the most important person you will ever need to know. As a reminder, here is your permission to shine.

Take a moment and notate the age old questions, who am I, what am I meant to be, what is my purpose. Then take a moment; think deep and answer those questions.

_____

_____

_____

_____

Chapter 6

Are you a Grown Responsible Woman?

Please don't be offended by the title, this is a legitimate question. First, let me remind you that the intent of this book is to help you become the best version of yourself. So to get you there, we must be open and honest with one another so that you can live unapologetically in "your truth." You will get through this, just as you have surpassed every other life issue, but this time, you have support. During the transition, you will be required to make a few decisions, which is vital to your success. How you end up, depends on how much you love and respect yourself!

So are you? Are you a responsible woman? Do you blame others for your shortcomings? Do you make excuses? Do you complain about lack? Are you a good Steward? Do you defer obligations for entertainment? Do you have a rainy day fund? Do you invest in your learning? Do you set appropriate boundaries? Are you a procrastinator? Do you plan for your future? I know this is a sensitive subject, and you may have never asked yourself these questions. Girlfriend, you are NOT alone, many of us have been where you are and from time to time, we still struggle. The important thing today is a new beginning and with a change of mindset, your future will reflect a Grown and Responsible Woman.

There are many reasons we are struggling financially. Some of it is due to immaturity and life events, such as divorce, job loss, death, bad money management, lack of knowledge, and materialism. Whatever the reason, we have found ourselves robbing Peter to pay Paul. Some of us are in so deep that a resolution is difficult to fathom. The rest of us, have no idea where to begin. How do we escape the pitfalls of debt and safely invest in living our best life?

My journey started about 5 years ago when my husband introduced to me, *Women and Money* by Suze Orman. Recognizing my financial habits, and seeing the potential, he felt like this book would really free me from being a "slave to sales." I read half of the book and thought it was doable. I began to "talk the talk" and suggest the reading to other ladies. I even took the "Stand in my truth" pledge. Sadly, it was all a hoax because I wasn't honest with myself. Saying the words, convicted me. Making a change for my husband, convicted me. Ensuring that I "saved" for our sons' future, convicted me. Being able to enjoy life, convicted me, but I wasn't ready to truly "stand in my truth." I would constantly undermine my progress by saying, "I worked hard, so why can't I have nice things?" Or, "at this price it's a steal." I constantly told myself little things to justify my buying. Little did I know that I was putting my self-respect on sale. I was deliberating forcing money to leave me and for what? None of the items ever added anything of value to me, nor did I learn anything from it. So I decided to truly read "Women and Money," only this time I finished the book.

Soon after, my husband and I sat down at the kitchen table to discuss how to tackle our finances and ensure that we were on the SAME page. A little transparency here, my husband has an accountant background, and I have, "I am the only girl, and I am used to getting my way" background; so getting us to a table to discuss finances was an accomplishment in itself. Needless to say, this was the beginning of many meetings to get our Finances on track.

Addressing our finances gave us a peace of mind, but for me, it also revealed opportunities for character reconstruction. I found out that I didn't like myself that much, and I was unhappy with the person I had become. I realized that I was insecure, and my view of my life was a façade. I also discovered that I was envious of people that had more than me. I didn't want to keep up with the Joneses;

I wanted to be the Joneses. The worst thing wasn't that I had lived with this situation so long but that I had projected those insecurities onto our sons. At first, I was devastated; but after deciding to change my viewpoint (mind), our finances, I knew that I could change my interactions with our sons.

Stewardship

Webster Dictionary defines stewardship as *the conducting, supervising, or managing of something;* **especially:** *the careful and responsible management of something entrusted to one's care.* Romans 3:23 (NIV) says for all have sinned and fall short of the glory of God. When I think of stewardship, I think of this verse and then I think of Grace.

Grace affords us the opportunity to begin again. Regardless of our past financial indiscretions, we can become good stewards starting today. The most challenging part is internal; it begins in the mind. First, we have to change the way we view money and its importance. The truth is, MONEY is important; it is a **resource** needed to sustain your desired way of life. Secondly, we must align our finances with our talents, for example, if you love to write; then write blogs, articles, and short works for magazines, and other publications. This is one way to obtain a revenue by doing something you enjoy. Thirdly, learn financial principles, they will help you to maintain your standards of living and allow you to participate in the Universal Law of Giving and Receiving.

Empowerment Technique

I empower you to recognize that you are a Good Steward. Embracing your responsibility and power to attract and retain money by changing your thought patterns and process. It is important to recognize that the way we allocate our time, effort, and money speaks volumes about what's important to our heart, giving us insight into our own personal development. Here are a few affirmations that can

assist you with right thinking.

- *There is No lack, limitation or Failure in my finances.*
- *I am a strong magnet to all types of currency and resources to be a blessing.*
- *I have more than enough to be a positive change in my world.*
- *I am a role model for my children, and they will learn sound financial principles from me.*
- *I am not limited by money and will attract all everything I need to live life abundantly.*

Review the affirmations above and then construct your own

affirmations to repeat below daily.

_____

_____

_____

_____

Chapter 7

A Field of Flowers

For beautiful eyes, look for the good in others;
for beautiful lips, speak only words
of kindness; and for poise, walk with the
knowledge that you are never alone.
Audrey Hepburn

Don't you just love flowers? They create a feeling of warmth, appreciation, gratitude, happiness, and love. Flowers come in all shapes, sizes, aromas, and colors and is appropriate for any occasions. Whether it is a get well plant, or bouquet of roses, a vase of iris or a planter of dahlias; all are beautiful and uniquely made. About 5 years ago, Ma Hellen, (my mother in law) introduced me to gardening. At first, I was hesitant, but her knowledge of each plant inspired me. Finally, I said to myself, how can I fail if she is here to help me, needless to say, she provided an adult reason for me to play in the dirt and I loved doing it. I get an absolute joy from watching flowers, plants, and vegetables grow into beautiful bright colors.

The diversity of flowers is just like the diversity in Women. We come in all varieties, which include but not limited to shape, size, creed, ethnicity, religion, age, and profession. All throughout history, women have been noted for achieving the unimaginable, and even though our recognition have been slow in making national news, there is no limit to our accomplishments. James E. Faust wrote, one of humankind's greatest blessings is for righteous womanhood to hold "the highest place of honor in human life" and to be "the perfect workmanship of God."

Everyday Life

Now that you have squared off with fear, anxiety, depression, hate, unforgiveness, and procrastination, you may feel lighter than before. Your steps are purposeful, and your words are deliberate. You are no longer existing but creating. You are a witness to the wind that brushes across your face, and you flirt with the sun as it dawns for the day. You have arrived, and the Universe has awakened all things for your good as you command the morning. Do you like that? I thought you would.... You have become a force to be reckoned with, but you are not alone. The Sisterhood is real, and together, possibilities are endless.

Business

On the journey of self-realization and fulfillment, it is important to surround ourselves with like-minded sisters. Proverbs 15:22 shares without consultation, plans are frustrated, but with many counselors they succeed. Establishing a personal and professional network of women will provide you with guidance, insight, and education. We must connect with women that have done that, been there and bought the T-shirt and can mentor you to avoid the pitfalls of business in your desired field. Collaboration and promotion of your sisters' gifts and talents helps them achieve the "highest place of honor" whether it is in the Church, in the home, in business or the world. So to get the most out of your "flower arrangement," you must be open to receive feedback from your network of experts. Your sisterhood's valuable insight can help to change perceptions and stereotypes about Women in your area of interest. They can help to motivate, sustain, influence, and ground you if necessary.

Friends, Foes, and Family Members

It would be an injustice to share the possibilities and not warn you about the challenges. Once you implement changes in how you think and what you do, it will not be long before your family and friends see the changes as well. Typically, you would assume they would be happy that you're taking control of your life, but that is not always the case. Just like with any other change, you will have resistance. The impact that resistance will have on your life, business, and relationship is based on how you manage the process. So when considering your family and friends, please keep in mind, their mindset is not on the same level as yours, so it may be hard for them to understand all the changes you are making and the reasons why. The ideal situation would be for you all to go through the process together, but if not, then you have to help them understand why, how, and when the changes are occurring. First and foremost, communication is essential so don't assume because you know them, the process would be easy and effortless. You will be surprised. It's not to say they won't be happy for you; it is to say change isn't easy, and communication before, during, and after the process is detrimental to your relationships.

As Creators, every experience affords us the opportunity to gain clarity about who we are personally and professionally as well as increase our self-worth.

Empowerment Technique

I empower you to create a network of like-minded individuals to help strengthen and promote your area of influence. Think about how the collaboration can be beneficial for all involved. Go online and review the Meetup Groups in your area and then write below the groups you can visit to begin the networking process. If one is not available, start one.

I also employ you to have an intimate conversation with your family and friends. Talk about your end goal and the work that is required to get you there. Express your need for their patience and support as you go through the process. To help with that conversation, write the areas you would need their support.

_____

_____

_____

_____

Chapter 8

Getting to know you

As we travel through life, we yearned to be coupled. A life partner is a special someone that understands, respects, and loves us; with the added benefit of sharing memorable moments, quality time, and overcoming life's issues, together. **Caveat**... life partners are individuals that you are DESTINED to be with; (equally yoked), not your cheating boyfriend or ex-husband, or baby daddy, your best friend turned boyfriend that should have stayed a best friend, your one-night stand that made you a mother or some other situation you didn't ask for or need and on and on and on. Remember, we are on the path to living life abundantly so no one from your past should be inappropriately labeled.

The Creation of Woman

Genesis 2:23-24 shares - *23rd The man said, "This is now bone of my bones, And flesh of my flesh; She shall be called Woman, Because she was taken out of Man." 24th - For this reason a man shall leave his father and his mother, and be joined to his wife; and they shall become one flesh.* Interesting personification, leaving your parents to become one flesh or one person; but based on today's divorce rate, many of us really don't know what "one flesh" means. If we looked at it from a physical, spiritual (intellectual), mental, and social position, we would realize that it all yields the same result or produce the same outcome. Before we discuss that outcome, let's talk about your ability to choose a "life partner."

Too Soon

Many women are hurt from relationships because they failed to get to know their suitor. If you are dating, please,

please, understand that you are more than a pretty face, a nice figure or a lovely smile. YOU are a Queen, and talk is cheap, including compliments. Even if you have known the person all of your life, it is super important to take things slow. Get to know them, which is more than 6 months to a year. The truth is, everyone has an alter ego, which is who you meet first. Generally, it takes 18 months before the curtain comes down and the real person shows up, plus any ingenious person would have resigned by then, so wait them out. Be smart, don't put yourself in situations that leave you vulnerable and at their mercy. If you see signs, don't ignore them, have enough confidence in yourself to exit the friendship. Stay in tune with yourself and take 1 day at a time, as this would remove the revolving door of bad relationships.

Soul Ties

Contracts, vows, agreements, labels, and promises are all a form of soul ties. Soul ties are created when souls are interweaved together in the spiritual realm, becoming one flesh. A soul tie can be formed in many ways, but the most common is through sexual relations. They are powerful and deadly at the same time. For example, you can meet someone and become intrigued based on an outward perception, such as attractiveness, being funny, or famous. After spending time with this individual, you may engage in agreement, whether it is to date, go shopping on Wednesday or hang out on Friday evenings; thus creating a soul tie. This may go on for months, even years but for whatever reason at some point the relationship dissolves, but the soul ties still exist until you break them. Godly soul ties are when husband and wives are attracted to each other; while ungodly soul ties can attract a woman of domestic violence to the man that abused and raped her; even though she can't stand him. This should be enough for you to take your time in getting to know potential life partners without involving sex. Soul ties must be broken in order to free yourself to bond with your Destined life partner. It can be a deciding factor in whether your relationship is a success or failure.

Candidates

So, back to Life Partners, if we think about where we were 5, 10, 15 years ago, you have to wonder why anyone would want to be with you? You were either damaged goods, unsure of yourself, carrying cancerous grudges, unable to forgive, stuck in yesterday or longing for it, devaluing yourself, financially irresponsible, unable to ask for what you wanted because you didn't know, and unaware of your talent and gifts. Look at yourself today; you are a Secure, Responsible, Forgiving, Self-Motivating, Educated, Knowledgeable, Forward-thinking, Understanding,

Assertive, Entrepreneur of a Woman. You are not the same as you were 5, 10, 15 years ago, and your approach to life issues aren't either. You realized that any and everyone in your life requires the same scrutiny you put yourself through over the last 8 Chapters. You have identified what you want and have put plans in place to achieve it. It would be out of character and downright insulting for you to let a potential Life Partner candidate sabotage all that you have worked for. As rigorous as the process is to get to know yourself, you must perform the same process when getting to know a potential life partner. I know that what I am sharing requires a mindset change, but your future is too important to stop or turn back now.

A Life Partner

Again, I ask why would anyone want you? It's not a trick question. Actually it's simple, you are the bone of their bone and flesh of their flesh. When your Life Partner happened upon you, they felt 2 things, an emptiness and a relief. The emptiness from, "this is who I have been missing all my life" and a relief that they finally found you. Of course, it is a journey, but once they get over the societal memes, they are ready to do what is needed to earn you, love you, and cherish you. If you are living your life fully aware, then you understand the commitment of having a life partner and willing to embrace the work that goes along with it. If we looked at it from a physical, spiritual (intellectual), mental, and social position, we would realize that it all yields the same result or produce the same conclusion. The conclusion that life is better connected, with 2 adults striving for the same goal; which is to live life abundantly together.

Empowerment Technique

I employ you to take your time in your relationships and allow yourself the opportunity to truly meet the person behind the mask. In the spirit of protecting your future, ask direct questions and expect answers. Be mindful of the signs and respond accordingly. I empower you to break soul ties with individuals of your past by renouncing them and the act. Once you have broken the soul ties, write the qualities and characteristics of your desired Life Partner below.

_____

_____

_____

_____

Chapter 9

Interruptions and Distractions

Do you remember when I shared that I was an optimist? Well, I am also a realist, and it's important to share life's interruptions and distractions. You see, they can come in any form and at any time. Interruptions and distractions have only one purpose in mind, and it is to derail you from your goal. They sit and wait while watching for the perfect moment to say, "excuse me, you forgot about me, and I need your attention. **RIGHT NOW**!"

If you don't recognize them, you will fall prey to their shenanigans. Once you adopt the mindset of empowerment and talent utilization, you become a target. So how do you deal or prepare for interruptions and distractions? First, let's identify a few types of interruptions and distractions.

The first one is internal. It can be as simple as thinking too much... you are so focused on doing a good job that you can't, because you are constantly thinking about doing a good job. This impedes your ability to act. Joyce Meyers shares in the Battlefield of the Mind, that the battle begins and end in the mind. The mind can create distractions such as daydreaming, over analyzing, depression, procrastination, and perfectionism to name a few. If you find yourself wrestling with internal conversations, go back and read how to practice the empowerment techniques of Chapter 3, Equipped for the journey to stop the culprits' dead in their tracks so that you can get back to business.

The next interruption or distraction is created by external factors. These cause the biggest conflict because they usually involve our loved ones and seem to be out of our control. Most of the time, they required financial and physical obligations that directly impact the goals we have set for ourselves. We rather see ourselves without than ignore the opportunity to aid someone we love, especially if it's within our power to do so. Depending on the situation, you should determine if the risks of not being there for someone else outweighs the benefit of being there for yourself. True discernment is a must.

In May of this year, around 6 a.m., I was preparing to attend a networking event in Charlotte, North Carolina, where I would have the opportunity to interface with authors, coaches, and other like-minded individuals. In the midst of getting ready to leave, I received a phone call from my son that his car was stolen the night before. As a mother, my heart dropped to the bottom of my chest and immediately I wanted to go to his aid. Even though my son had decided to leave home and live in his car for 2 months, I still wanted to SAVE him. My flight was scheduled to leave at 1 p.m. that afternoon, so I had to make a decision and answer questions to appease my heart. Should I stay and try to help him through this situation or should I go and potentially set the stage for my writing career? If I stay, what message would I be sending my son? What message would I be sending myself? So I decided to push my flight back to 5 p.m. that afternoon and picked up my son. We put him in a hotel for the 2 nights that I would be away and promised to assist when I returned from my event. My decision to move forward with my plans set the stage for my son's independence and relinquished my need to nurture him. Needless to say, my writing career was initiated, and my son had started the journey to becoming the Man he was destined to be. Due to prayer and supplication, his car was retrieved the next day, undamaged.

Interruptions and Distractions are all around in our everyday life. Mark 4:19 shares, but all too quickly the message is crowded out by the worries of this life, the lure of wealth, and the desire for other things, so no fruit is produced. This verse is referring to distractions and how things can keep us preoccupied or steal our focus so that our attention is diverted. We allow problems, situations, and events of our life as well as others' to keep us tied up and unaware of what's important or right; which delays us from our purpose. Please don't misunderstand me, some situations require you to be present and involved, but you must count up the cost, and **you and you alone** should determine the worth. The ultimate message of The Woman's Blueprint is that you set the rules for your life and be the author of the dictionary that defines you.

Empowerment Technique

I employ you to keep a journal of all the times that you experience interruptions and distractions from your planned objectives. Determine the value and the cost associated with your involvement. Write them down. Based on your notes below decide if your life is in balance or if a change is in order.

For example:

Event	Cost	Impact
Planned Trip	$1200	Planned objective
Son's stolen car	$357	Interruption

In the situation above, the benefit of my planned trip outweighed the theft of my son's car. Although, he received the necessary support and the opportunity to grieve without a 1000 questions. It was a distraction that could have caused me a business opportunity. Again, all situations require discernment and wisdom, had it been a different situation, a different decision would have been made.

_____

_____

_____

_____

Chapter 10

Thank you

Thank you for your respect. Thank you for being supportive of my happiness, my relationships, my dreams, and my dignity. Thank you for being compassionate and understanding when I'm having a bad day. Thank you for thinking of me and others as often as you do. Thank you for being there whenever you're needed. Thank you for always giving that extra push. Thank you for talking things out even when it's uncomfortable and uneasy. Thank you for meeting me halfway. Thank you for making time. Thank you for no excuses, no lies, and no broken promises. Thank you for your full presence. Thank you for comforting the pain in my eyes while everyone else still believes the smile on my face. Thank you for not judging and being extra kind and patience. Thank you for not treating me like you know me better than I know myself. Thank you for being willing to be wrong. Thank you for being there through good times and bad. Thank you for understanding that I can't always be strong. Thank you for facing problems with me. Thank you for going out of your way, even when it's not convenient. Thank you for actually wanting to be there for me. Thank you for walking the talk and believing in me. Thank you for encouraging me when I stumble. Thank you for using caring words. Thank you for accepting me just the way I am. Thank you for making me feel comfortable in my skin. Thank you for simply enjoying my company. Thank you for valuing my time. Thank you for showing me that you are grateful to have me in your life. Thank you for supporting me in making myself a priority. Thank you for sincerely loving me and helping me love myself more too. Thank you for all the little things you do that make a big difference. Thank you for being patient and forgiving when I step on your toes. Thank you for not holding my unchangeable past against me. Thank you for not expecting our relationship to always be easy. Thank you for giving me the solitude and space I need.

And most of all, thank you for being YOU.

Isn't she lovely? Isn't she wonderful...
Stevie Wonder

To reiterate, the intent of this book is to celebrate, empower and share with you the things that are robbing us from fulfilling our purpose and prohibiting us from living an abundant life. You deserve to be and live in the best version of YOU. It does not matter what your current situation is or what has kept you from achieving your goals. Now is the time, here is the place, and you are the person that will make it happen. So renew your mind and transform into the Blueprint of the Woman you were meant to be.

I cannot wait to meet you.

NOTES

Dyer, W. (2009). Excuses Begone! Carlsbad, CA: Hay House USA

Stanley, S. (2015). Comparison Trap. Alpharetta, GA: North Point Ministries, Inc.

Trimm, C. (2007). Commanding Your Morning. Lake Mary, FL: Charisma House

Rath, T. (2007). StrengthsFinder 2.0. New York, NY: Gallup Press

Ruiz, Don, (1997). The Four Agreements. San Rafael, CA: Amber-Allen

Meyer, J. (2002). Battlefield of the Mind. New York, NY: Warner Faith

Amen, D. (1999) Change your Brain, Change your Life. New York, NY: Three River Press

Lipton, B. (2005) Biology of Belief. Carlsbad, CA: Hay House USA

Orman, S. (2010) Women and Money. New York, NY: Spiegel & Grau.

Allen, J. (2001) As a Man Thinketh. Mechanicsburg, PA: Tremendous Life Books

(1996) The Bible. New International Version. Tyndale House Publishers, Inc.

ABOUT THE AUTHOR

Elizabeth D Wallace is a highly inspired author and speaker, who is passionate about helping women discover the best version of themselves. Elizabeth was born in Mount Vernon, GA on July 24, 1971 as Elizabeth D Robinson. She graduated from Vidalia High School in May 1989, and from American Intercontinental University (AIU) in Atlanta with a Bachelor of Arts in HR Management in May 2007. She remained at AIU to complete her Masters of Science degree in Operations Management in May 2009. Prior to receiving her education, Elizabeth worked at US Customs in Washington DC from 1991-1995, holding various HR positions. Desiring to be closer to her parents, she relocated to Atlanta, Ga as a US Customs Inspector until 2001.

After the birth of her youngest son, she decided to join the corporate world in the HR arena. Where she served as a Professional Human Resource Consultant, and as a member of several networking groups. It was not long before she discovered her professional and personal interests was to motivate women to understand their purpose by recognizing their natural born gifts and talents. Fostering an inclusive and empowering environment in the workplace, she used compassion and personal candor, to inspire individuals to initiate purpose and maximize their full potential. Elizabeth currently lives in Atlanta, GA with her husband and 3 sons. This is her first published book.

For more information please visit:
www.elizabethwallaced.com
www.thewomansblueprint.com

Made in the USA
Columbia, SC
24 June 2023

18792101R00067